THE FOUR PHASES OF CREATIVITY

A Path to Unleashing the Natural
Flow of Your Creativity

Dedicated to
Love, the Moon and Mother Nature.
Thank you for showing me the way to
a more relaxed, simpler lifestyle.

This book was created with the support of my patrons at patreon.com/elinap and a grant from The Finnish Illustration Association. Thank you so much!

Third edition
Copyright © 2022 elinap - Elina Puohiniemi
All Rights Reserved. No part of this book may be reproduced in whole or
in part in any form without prior written permission of the publisher.
Publisher: elinap, Vantaa, Finland
Design & illustrations: elinap
ISBN: 978-952-67473-4-7

Imagine a life where your creativity
flows freely and naturally!

One joyful project after another comes to fruition, and you
feel accomplished and nourished by your life.

Let's look at the big picture together.
Welcome to the journey with us!

Creativity is all about making your dream come true.
It starts with a vision or an idea that turns into a project with your help. At its
best, it's like planting a seed, nurturing it and watching it grow until it bears fruit.
Before you know it, you get to pick the fruit and enjoy it!

The creative cycle of any project or dream follows the same rhythm as the four
seasons in nature. The four phases of the moon have the same qualities as the
four seasons. And even the times of the day follow the same rule:

Start refreshed in the morning,
take action during the day,
and then rest at night.
When every action step required for creation has its place,
creativity flows and life feels more effortless.

Showing up for your dream is all you need to do
when you know how to show up and when.

Respecting rest in between all the efforts you make may feel rebellious in the world we live in, but that's what it takes when you want to follow your heart.

Rest is mentioned a lot throughout the book, and each time it's an invitation from your heart to **rest in joy**. Sometimes it's sleep, sometimes dancing, but one thing is for sure: Resting connects you to creativity and your heart.
Keep coming back to things you love and need to do.

If you are too busy to rest, hearing your heart's whispers becomes really challenging. Thus, rest is the most important step to take first,
so you'll be able to hear what she has to say.
She knows which dreams to go for!

Your dream is the seed. Your life is the soil. Your dream
chose you, and it deserves to be nurtured.

Let's first meet our guides—Mira, her heart and the moon—before diving into what nature and the seasons have to say about the path to
natural flow of creativity.

MEET THE CHARACTERS

MIRA is an ever-curious, joyful inner child who loves to follow her heart and doesn't stop, even when the ego butts in (the ego is the part of us that wants to play it safe and keep going). She determinedly finds a way to understand the situation more deeply. The drama of her life builds up around this one question: *Will she choose what her ego tells her to do, or will she keep following her heart?*

MIRA'S HEART represents inner guidance, intuition, inner wisdom, soul or true self—choose whatever word you want to use. She symbolizes the love that we are. A love that is all-encompassing, all-accepting. She knows our birthright is Joy, Love, and Ease. We all have the power to choose to follow our heart. We just need to pause, look around and remember that Love is ever-present. The heart never leaves Mira's side even if she loses sight of it. Love will stick around like the Sun. Clouds may hide it but it still shines. To make choosing love easier for you, try expressing gratitude or acts of kindness. A tiny smile offered to a stranger is a start!

THE MOON represents the feminine creative energy. Having the moon guide you to embrace the four phases of the creative cycle brings you peace and helps you take purposeful action that fills you up from inside.

OTHER SYMBOLS USED IN THIS BOOK

A HEART-SHAPED SEED represents your dream that grows with time and as you show up for it.

LOTS OF LITTLE HEARTS represent other people who are pure love—just like you are, too.

STARS symbolize miracles, which are shifts in perception according to *A Course in Miracles*. When Mira looks back on her journey, she can see all those miracle moments she got to experience.

All creative processes start
with a dream.

Whether creative expression happens in nature or in your mind, it doesn't show up on the surface right away. Its roots are growing sturdy in the dark, beneath the surface.

TRUST THE CALLING TO CREATE AND TAKE THE FIRST STEP.

SPRING wakes nature up from its rest, and soon all that is ready to show up, sprouts into the open.

**BE PATIENT AND
TRUST IN DIVINE TIMING.**

Nature never rushes, every little living thing has a schedule of its own
to grow, to bloom, and to bear fruit or otherwise impact the whole.

**MAKE SURE NOTHING STANDS IN THE WAY
—NOT EVEN YOURSELF.
TAKE GOOD CARE OF YOUR OWN WELLBEING.**

Having space to grow and being healthy becomes essential,
especially in the middle of the abundance of SUMMER.

**ENJOY THE FRUITS AND CELEBRATE!
REFLECT BACK AND TAKE IT ALL IN TO BE PREPARED FOR
YOUR NEXT CREATIVE ENDEAVOR.**

AUTUMN comes and so does the time of harvest. It's time to let go. Nature does this gracefully by gathering all she needs for the next round of creative expression and letting go of everything that no longer serves her.

Now it's time to rest.

ALLOW YOURSELF TO PAUSE.

That's what nature does in WINTER, too.

But when you are an overwhelmed human being, with dozens of tasks at hand, how do you reset and start following nature's guidance?

It all begins with and always goes back to knowing how to
CONNECT WITH YOUR HEART. (See page 21)

Then **ASK THE MOON FOR HELP!** The four phases of the moon have
the same qualities as the seasons. (Her guidance starts on page 24.)

GET TO KNOW YOUR OWN RHYTHMS. Paying attention to where you are
at with your own rhythms and creative flow is empowering. (See page 22.)

Experiment and **GIVE YOURSELF TIME AND GRACE**
to get there eventually. (See page 23.)

If you need more clarity on how to nurture
your dream, take out your journal and
go through **THE JOURNALING PROMPTS**
of the phase you are in.
(See pages 29, 39, 49, 59.)

In case you feel lost at any phase, you can look for the
illustrated **TROUBLESHOOTING** tips and find solutions
to the most common bumps on the path.
(See pages 30, 40, 50, 60.)

Overwhelm, feeling stuck, depression, and being in
the vicious cycle of always striving but never arriving
can cause frustration in your life when you are creating
something new.

Becoming aware and paying attention to the challenges in each phase
of creativity will help you BLISSFULLY step into the flow of life.

It takes a while to get used to syncing your creativity with the natural rhythms of
life and finding out what works for you, but in the end, it will bring you so much
more peace and simplicity that it's worth it!

Enjoy the journey of resetting and
returning to the natural rhythm of life
one step at a time!

THE DIFFERENCE BETWEEN EGO-DRIVEN GOALS AND SOUL-FULFILLING DREAMS

When you undervalue rest and you have a need to do more and be on the go at all times, constant running around could make ego your running buddy. That's when your dreams and goals become complicated and unaligned with your truth. Appearance may be more important than fulfillment. The whole process may feel like constant pushing, and it becomes really difficult. The ego goals you achieve may not fulfill you, but instead they leave you wanting for more. Trying to succeed by achieving ego goals looks very different from the path introduced in this book. Let's commit to following the heart instead!

And remember, even behind every ego-driven dream there is a feeling you wish your dream would bring. Is it Joy, Peace, Freedom, or something else? Dig deep and look for a feeling you want to add into your life. When you do this, you will not need to dwell on what your dream should look like. You will know how it feels, and you will recognize it when that feeling arrives!

When you concentrate on the feeling you desire, not the appearance of it, something better may come your way.

HOW TO CONNECT WITH YOUR HEART

If you feel uncertain about what the right dream for
you is, whether you hear the whispers of your heart
or fear you're facing an ego-driven goal, the answer
is to **rest in joy**. Here is how to do it:

Ask yourself:
- "What brings me joy?" and then go do it!
  It can be a nature walk, creating art, watching the sunset, hugging your
  loved ones, gardening, dancing, laughing at a funny TV show…
  Anything that makes you smile and feel lighter.
- "What am I grateful for?"
  Make a list in your head or write it out in a journal.
- "What does resting in joy mean for me in this moment?"

Sit with these questions and just let the answers come. If it feels difficult,
look back and remind yourself of the last time you laughed and felt lighter.
What were you doing then? Who were you with?
Is it possible to do something similar now? Go do it!

When you feel refreshed and joyful, ask yourself what your dream is.
The response is now more likely to be aligned with your heart.

A NOTE TO WOMEN WHO BLEED

Your menstrual cycle has the same qualities and energies as the phases of the moon and the four seasons. Usually your own inner cycle overruns nature's external cycles, so don't worry if the forces of nature are not exactly synced up with your period, instead learn to turn inward and take notes from your own rhythms.

Listen to your own body and feel if the following applies to your life: It is easiest to turn inward and rest like nature does during the winter while you are bleeding. During ovulation, however, you may feel the most outward—it can feel like you're shining as brightly as the summer sun. And the closer you get to your period again, the easier it is to laser focus andfinish up what you started earlier in the cycle.

Embrace what your body tells you at certain times of the
month and let it guide you to which action(s) to take.

This way your body becomes your teacher
for the steps of the creative path.

A NOTE ON TIME

No matter how long the cycles are in nature (Moon cycles around the earth in about 28 days, the four seasons take a year to go through), your creative dream has a cycle of its own. In most cases you can't plan ahead on how long your dream will take to realize.

Each phase for your creative dream takes as long as it takes. It can be a morning, it can be a day, or it can be a month. The moon and the seasons are here to lay out a structure—the path—that you can follow to go through the phases so that your creativity can flow naturally.

Don't force your dream into a certain timeframe (that's what the ego would do). Rest well every night and start again refreshed in the morning.

Remember you started it by dreaming of it.
It is yours to celebrate eventually!
Believe in your dream and yourself and keep
the dream alive by showing up for it!
You and your dream deserve it.

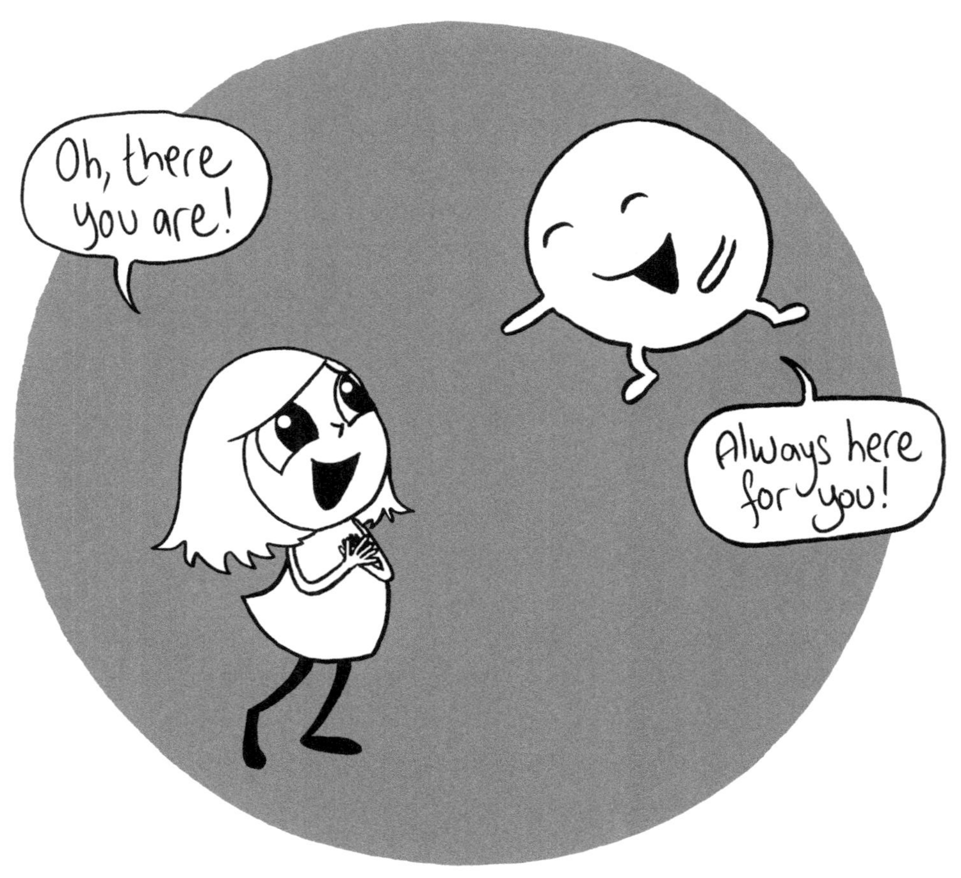

Whenever you're outside at night and the sky is clear,
look to the moon for guidance.

REST IN JOY & DREAM

SET INTENTIONS

PLANT THE SEEDS

NURTURE THE DREAM & SHINE LIGHT ON IT

ASK FOR HELP & COLLABORATE

TWEAK & PRUNE

TAKE FOCUSED ACTION

LET GO OF WHAT NO LONGER SERVES THE DREAM

FINISH WHAT YOU STARTED

HARVEST & REFLECT

CELEBRATE

NEW MOON, WINTER, NIGHT

REST IN JOY - DREAM - SET INTENTIONS

At the beginning, there is a dream. Start by giving your dream wings.
Let its roots grow. Use your imagination. Do nothing yet, just let it brew.
Feel into it and see if it's aligned with who you are.
Rest with it.

♥ How can I offer myself more rest today?

♥ Today what does resting in joy mean for me?

♥ What do I really want?

♥ What does my dream look and feel like?

♥ What feeling do I want to add more of into my life?

♥ What would make my life more meaningful/fun/easier?

♥ What excites me the most about my dream?

♥ What is the #1 piece of advice I can give myself for finishing what I start?

♥ Plan and schedule rest ahead of time:

How can I make sure I rest regularly throughout the process?

♥ Always when you pause to rest and turn inward with these questions,

set an intention for the period of time before your next planned rest.

Keep it simple, use 1-5 words for your intention.

Write it on a post-it note and keep it somewhere

where you can see it often.

FEELING LOST?

THE NEW MOON PHASE - A QUICK TIP

If you keep going without honoring rest, you will miss out on the wonderful opportunities to get connected with your inner wisdom and heart.
Rest now.

DIVE DEEPER INTO WHAT THE COMMON CHALLENGES IN THIS PHASE ARE AND HOW TO SOLVE THEM ON THE NEXT PAGES.

Feeling you need to force yourself into action?

Does it feel like you've tried everything, but nothing seems to work?

You have permission to rest and turn inward. It will help!

Sleep if that's what you need, or rest in JOY and go do something you love to do!

 **If you skipped steps in your last cycle of creativity, something may have been left on your to-do list. This makes it hard to proceed now or later during this new cycle.**

Struggling with procrastinating and doing anything else but following the path?

Look at your to-do list carefully and consider if it feels aligned. If not, do the exercise on page 21 to realign. Feel free to prune what no longer needs to be on the list. Refresh your dream. Is it still what you want? You can always go back and start again. Wherever you are, concentrate on the step you are taking right now. The next one will appear when it's ready.

… And don't skip any steps this time.

Just one step at a time.

 **Your cup is empty. There's nothing left to give.
You may even feel depressed.**

Feeling like you've got nothing left to give?

Trust that resting will fill you up.

Enjoy pausing for a moment.
Rest brings up treasures from deep within.

In case you feel emptiness AFTER you've made your dream come true, know that that's perfectly normal for a creative endeavor. It's a sign that you need to acknowledge your achievement. Celebrate and then rest. Bask in the glory of arrival for a while and let yourself be filled up with joy.

WAXING MOON, SPRING, MORNING

PLANT THE SEEDS

It's time to start taking action! Now you know your dream and what it looks like. It's like you have a beautiful seed that you can plant and start tending to. Take the first step and then continue, one step at a time.

♥ What does my dream need so it can grow?

♥ If life is the soil, what do I need to do to prepare my life for my dream?

♥ What represents light or sunshine for my dream?

♥ Who or what helps me keep going and showing up for my dream?

♥ What waters the seed of my dream?

♥ How can I nourish my dream when it's growing?

♥ How can I nurture the soil in which I've planted the seed of my dream?

♥ What clouds my dream - What doubts do I have about my dream?
Acknowledging your doubts is helpful so you can move on
and not give them power.

♥ What is the next right step
I can take for my dream?

FEELING LOST?

THE WAXING MOON PHASE - A QUICK TIP

If you scatter your attention to all the possible seeds you could plant, you will easily fluster yourself and miss out on being there for your dream. What happens when you don't show up? Nothing grows but weeds. Choose one dream and take action, one step at a time. Remember, your dream is the seed, your life is the soil, and your dream needs time, water and sun to grow.

DIVE DEEPER INTO WHAT THE COMMON CHALLENGES IN THIS PHASE ARE AND HOW TO SOLVE THEM ON THE NEXT PAGES.

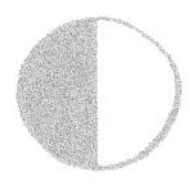 **Too many seeds have been planted. You have no way of proceeding with all of them. Your attention is just scattered everywhere.**

Enjoying an overflow of ideas and struggling with where to start?

Pick one dream and start there.

Give it your full attention. Which one does your heart favor? If you are bursting with ideas, gently jot them down. Choose only one to continue with now.
It'll pay you back big time. You can come back to the others later.

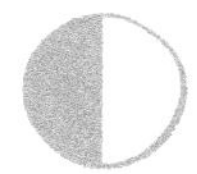 **The soil is sour. It may not be the right timing for the dream.**

Does it feel like your dream always escapes from you?

Start with tending the soil to make yourself and your life ready to receive.

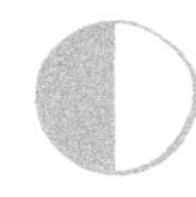 **There's not enough water to nourish your dream.
Something is blocking the flow.**

Having a creator's block?

Commit to taking baby steps, one
at a time, to tend to your dream.

Even a little bit
of attention IS
attention already,
and it waters
the seed.
Give your dream
enough attention
and nourishment,
and the more of what you
desire will show up in your life.

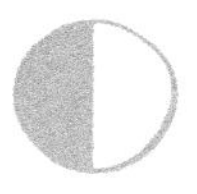 **It's too cloudy. Something is blocking the sun.**

Are you feeling hopeless and lost with your dream?

Concentrate on gratitude.

Gratitude is the light that pours in through the cracks in the clouds of your life. Ask yourself, "What am I grateful for?" and celebrate every action you take. It will help you clear the clouds. You've got this!

FULL MOON, SUMMER, MIDDAY

NURTURE & SHOW UP FOR YOUR DREAM - ASK FOR HELP -
COLLABORATE - TWEAK - LET GO

When the Sun lights up the moon, it's easy to see the bigger picture. Do the same and shine light on your dream to see where it's at right now and if there are some weeds around it that need to be removed before the next new moon. If you have gone solo with your dream so far, this is a good time to ask for help.

♥ Is there something about my dream I need or could tweak?

♥ How can I nurture my dream today?

♥ How can I offer extra loving care to my dream and myself over this time?

♥ What does my dream need today?

♥ What do I need?

♥ Who can help me with my dream?

♥ Is there something in my life that no longer serves me
and the person I want to become?

♥ Do I need to weed and let go of something?

♥ What is my next action step
for my dream to come true?

FEELING LOST?

THE FULL MOON PHASE - A QUICK TIP

If you are now at full speed, showing up here and there and everywhere—if you did end up planting more than you can handle—you may be at risk of burning yourself out. Forcing your dream to bloom seldom works. Instead, let it bloom effortlessly, in its natural time, and look for ways to nurture yourself and take it easy. Sleep more, eat healthy and spend time with your loved ones.
And always remember to ask for help!

DIVE DEEPER INTO WHAT THE COMMON CHALLENGES IN THIS PHASE ARE AND HOW TO SOLVE THEM ON THE NEXT PAGES.

◯ **Too much to do.**

Feeling like you don't have enough arms and legs to get it all done?

Sort through your to do list.
Get clear on your priorities.

What needs to be done? What can wait?
What can be delegated?
Who can you ask for help?

 **Too many others to please.**

*Never having time for
your own dreams?*

Put yourself first.
You deserve it!

Simple as that.
Butting into everyone
else's business is a real
distraction that can take
you away from finishing
what you started (and
then beating yourself
up afterwards).

 **Hiding yourself when it's obvious you need to show up.**

Struggling with putting yourself first and asking for what you need?

Pause and consider what you may need?

Do you need rest? Or maybe help?

You'll be surprised how much help there is available.

You just need to ask.

 **Feeling discouraged and doubting if your dream will ever come true.**

Does it feel like your dream will always stay a dream?

Your heart planted the seed in your life.
Trust her wisdom.

Your dream showed up for YOU so it belongs to YOU. Be proud of it and let it shine. It is in your life for a good reason! You'll discover that reason once the dream is realized.

WANING MOON, FALL, EVENING

FINISH WHAT YOU STARTED - HARVEST -
REFLECT - CELEBRATE

The last part of the creative cycle carries the powers of autumn: harvesting and preparing for the winter. The trees pull in what they need to bud again in the spring and let go of the rest by dropping their leaves. In your life this translates into celebrating the completion of your project, reflecting on what worked out, and holding onto only what you need to continue to the next project. At this phase you are able to laser focus on the task in front of you. Use this super power to your advantage to get where you want to be!

♥ What action steps do I need to take next
to finish what I started?

Once you are finished ask the following questions for reflection
and then celebrate!

♥ What went well?
♥ What actions were effortless for me?
♥ What strengths did I use?
♥ What did I learn and want to take in from this process?
♥ What do I no longer want to repeat in the next creative cycle?

♥ What can I celebrate and how will I celebrate
what I have accomplished?
♥ Who will I celebrate and
share this with?

FEELING LOST?

THE WANING MOON PHASE - A QUICK TIP

In case you haven't yet given your dream enough attention, this phase could turn into a stormy one. To avoid the hail and thunderstorm that can harm the growth and take you down, show up for your dream now. Ask what it needs so that it can get to the finish line and listen carefully to what it says.
You need each other now!

DIVE DEEPER INTO WHAT THE COMMON CHALLENGES IN THIS PHASE ARE AND HOW TO SOLVE THEM ON THE NEXT PAGES.

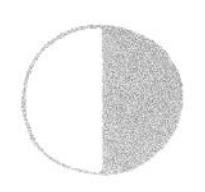 **Still too much to do. It's hard to focus.**

Terrified of the length of your to do list?

Drop your measuring stick and focus on the most important thing on your list.

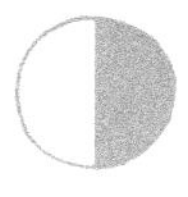 **Seeing the same old things happening and not making progress with your dream. It's like bumping into a wall.**

Feeling like you've seen this struggle before and it feels impossible to move past it?

When you notice a familiar pattern coming up, look back and take notes from your past. What is one thing you can learn from your past? There's no need to keep running into the wall again and again. Stick a loving reminder of what you've learnt on it and next time you'll be aware.

It's time to look back and learn.

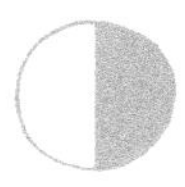 **Being very, very frustrated.**

Are you about to explode with frustration?

You are allowed to pause and breathe
at any given moment!
When is the last time you felt really rested and joyful?

After resting in joy, you can ask yourself, "What do I really want?" When your dream is aligned with your truth, it all becomes easier. Sometimes frustration hits when you have a burning desire to create, but haven't answered the call. Make a promise now to show up for your dream one step at a time. Use the excess energy that frustration brings to make space for your dream and take the first step.

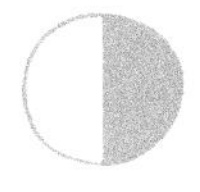 **Joining the comparison game, being frustrated in being stuck where you are with what you've got, and being "not there yet".**

Wondering why everyone else seems to do so much better?

Put on some blinders.

Do everything you need to stay on track and FINISH WHAT YOU HAVE STARTED!
It's your life and you already have all you need within you.

Focus on finishing your own thing.

 **Anxious to get it done. "Couldn't I be done with this already?"**

Struggling with getting to the finish line?

Recommit to your dream.

Remember that
all projects have
ebbs and flows.
Playing with

your heart for a while will
make it easier for you to
recommit.
Take a break and go do something
that lights you up.

Come back, recommit and continue.

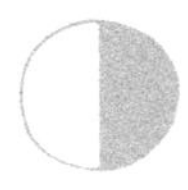 **Tempted to hop right into the next project now?**

Suffering from the shiny object syndrome?

Pause first and finish the cycle.

Look back and
see what worked out and
what you can learn from it.

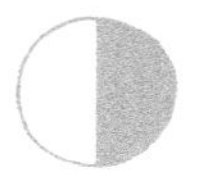 **In case your ego goals were not met.**

Upset that it didn't go as you planned?

Celebrate the work you did.
You learned so much.

When you examine your mistakes and/or failure with your heart, you can see it was part of a grander plan. Maybe it showed you that this is not where you were supposed to go. See it as a re-direction from your heart and trust that you will create something even more wonderful after this.

Look beyond the ego goal you had and ask yourself,
"What was I really after?"
You may be surprised that the feeling you really desired did pop up somewhere
else in your life. It may look different, but the feeling is there.
So you achieved it after all!

NOW LET'S CELEBRATE!

Celebrate! Share your accomplishment with your friends and the world! You can celebrate every step you take. The more you give yourself credit for having followed your heart, the more joyful the journey becomes. Who wouldn't want to continue on this path of increasing joy?

I want
some too!
Let's fill you
up first.

Then let yourself

REST IN JOY

for as long as it takes.

I wonder where that leads to...
Here we go again!

AND SOONER THAN YOU REALIZE,

You'll get curious again to see what's coming up ahead.

Now, with a rested mind and heart, you are ready for another new start!

Listen to your heart and let her lead you to your
next wonderful adventure one step at a time for
now you know what to do!

REFLECTIONS ON RESTING & DREAMING

What are the most loving, thought-provoking insights you had on your journey when it comes to resting and dreaming?

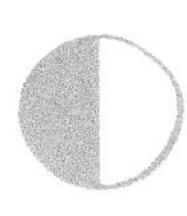

INSIGHTS FOR NEW BEGINNINGS

What useful, uplifting ideas did you have for taking the first steps in inviting something new into your life?

 IDEAS FOR SHOWING UP FOR YOUR DREAM

Make a list of the ways that help you show up for your dream
in a sweet and sustainable way.

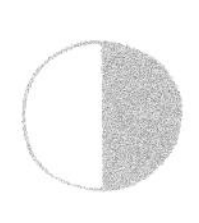

WISDOM FOR FINISHING WHAT YOU START

What was the most helpful mindset shift or idea you had that will help you get to the finish line with your dream?

DOODLING MIRACLES
- INSPIRING JOY & REFLECTION -

Mira(cle)Doodles are illustrations from a spiritual path,
born from a need to question the ego's ways and to
follow the heart no matter what comes your way.
Inspired by inner musings about life, they simplify and
explain life's struggles and spiritual challenges with a loving
twist—They show how it's possible to choose Love and
be at peace in any moment.

The doodles help you connect with your own inner wisdom
and inspire you to expand into a deeper understanding of
life and Love.

ABOUT THE AUTHOR & ILLUSTRATOR

Elina Puohiniemi, aka elinap, is an artist, life coach and the creator of the Mira(cle)Doodles series. She loves to sing her soul song to the trees on her daily forest walks and follow her happy poodle's wagging tail. When it gets dark out she looks for the moon to see what phase she's in and searches for a loving meaning in everything she experiences. As a tactile learner she needs to draw what she wants to understand, and thus were born her uplifting doodles that simplify and explain spiritual challenges with a loving twist.
She lives in Finland with her husband and their two teenage sons.
And the poodle of course.

ACKNOWLEDGMENTS

The Four Phases of Creativity was inspired by my own inner journey into creativity as well as my studies of the moon phases, the seasons and cyclical living. I'm deeply grateful to my grandma for introducing nature's wisdom and the power of the moon to me early in my childhood and to my mom for showing me how to track my period from the beginning. My thanks also go to Gabriela Ariana for inspiring me to truly step into this journey, and Kate Northrup and her Origin Membership for further exploring it together.

9 789526 747347